Aran Pillows to CROCHET

Classic and timeless, Aran pillows are the perfect accessories for every décor! Becky Stevens designed the seven crochet patterns with plenty of interesting textures, mostly from simple post stitches. The pillows are sized to fit 24" or 14" pillow forms, so finishing is also a breeze. They're wonderful for housewarming gifts!

Meet Becky Stevens

Becky Stevens made the move from her home state of Pennsylvania to Maryland 41 years ago—which was about the time she started crocheting. She's learned so much about the skill since then that she teaches a weekly group in her home.

"Our informal get-togethers are great for helping my friends learn crochet," says Becky. "In turn, they help me prepare for teaching crochet at a lake resort in New York.

"The most rewarding things about crochet," Becky says, "are relaxing with your project and seeing the final result, whether you make it for yourself or as a very personal, thoughtful gift."

LEISURE ARTS, INC.
Little Rock, Arkansas

Basketweave Center Pillow

Shown on page 5.

■■□□ EASY +

Finished Size: 23" (58.5 cm) square

MATERIALS
Medium Weight Yarn (4)
[7 ounces, 364 yards
(198 grams, 333 meters) per skein]:
  3 skeins
Crochet hook, size G (4 mm) **or** size needed
  for gauge
24" (61 cm) Square pillow form, knife-edge

GAUGE: 14 sc and 16 rows = 4" (10 cm)

Gauge Swatch: 4" (10 cm) square
Ch 15.
Row 1: Sc in second ch from hook and in each ch across: 14 sc.
Rows 2-16: Ch 1, turn; sc in each sc across. Finish off.

✳✳

STITCH GUIDE

FRONT POST HALF DOUBLE CROCHET
  (abbreviated FPhdc)
YO, insert hook from **front** to **back** around post of st indicated *(Fig. 1, page 23)*, YO and pull up a loop, YO and draw through all 3 loops on hook.

BACK POST HALF DOUBLE CROCHET
  (abbreviated BPhdc)
YO, insert hook from **back** to **front** around post of st indicated *(Fig. 1, page 23)*, YO and pull up a loop, YO and draw through all 3 loops on hook.

FRONT POST DOUBLE CROCHET
  (abbreviated FPdc)
YO, working in **front** of previous row, insert hook from **front** to **back** around post of st indicated *(Fig. 3, page 23)*, YO and pull up a loop even with loops on hook (3 loops on hook), (YO and draw through 2 loops on hook) twice. Skip st behind FPdc.

FRONT POST CLUSTER
  (abbreviated FPcl) (uses one st)
★ YO, working in **front** of previous row, insert hook from **front** to **back** around post of st indicated *(Fig. 3, page 23)*, YO and pull up a loop even with loops on hook, YO and draw through 2 loops on hook; repeat from ★ once **more**, YO and draw through all 3 loops on hook. Skip st behind FPcl.

POPCORN (uses one sc)
4 Dc in sc indicated, drop loop from hook, insert hook from **front** to **back** in first dc of 4-dc group, hook dropped loop and draw through st *(Fig. 2, page 23)*.

FRONT
Ch 82.

Row 1 (Right side)**:** Sc in second ch from hook and in each ch across: 81 sc.

Note: Loop a short piece of yarn around any stitch to mark Row 1 as **right** side.

Row 2: Ch 1, turn; sc in each sc across.

Row 3: Ch 1, turn; sc in first 4 sc, work FPdc around sc one row **below** each of next 2 sc, sc in next sc, work FPdc around sc one row **below** each of next 2 sc, † sc in next 3 sc, work FPdc around sc one row **below** next sc, sc in next 5 sc, work FPcl around sc one row **below** next sc, sc in next sc, work FPcl around sc one row **below** next sc, sc in next 5 sc, work FPdc around sc one row **below** next sc, sc in next 3 sc †, work FPhdc around each of next 3 sts, (work BPhdc around each of next 3 sts, work FPhdc around each of next 3 sts) 3 times, repeat from † to † once, work FPdc around sc one row **below** each of next 2 sc, sc in next sc, work FPdc around sc one row **below** each of next 2 sc, sc in last 4 sc.

Row 4: Ch 1, turn; sc in first 30 sts, work BPhdc around each of next 3 sts, (work FPhdc around each of next 3 sts, work BPhdc around each of next 3 sts) 3 times, sc in last 30 sts.

Row 5: Ch 1, turn; sc in first 4 sc, skip first 2 FPdc one row **below**, work FPdc around each of next 2 FPdc, sc in next sc, working in **front** of FPdc just made, work FPdc around each skipped FPdc one row **below**, † sc in next 3 sc, work FPdc around next FPdc one row **below**, sc in next 4 sc, work FPcl around FPcl one row **below**, sc in next 3 sc, work FPcl around next FPcl one row **below**, sc in next 4 sc, work FPdc around next FPdc one row **below**, sc in next 3 sc †, work FPhdc around each of next 3 sts, (work BPhdc around each of next 3 sts, work FPhdc around each of next 3 sts) 3 times, repeat from † to † once, skip next 2 FPdc one row **below**, work FPdc around each of next 2 FPdc, sc in next sc, working in **front** of FPdc just made, work FPdc around each skipped FPdc one row **below**, sc in last 4 sc.

Row 6: Ch 1, turn; sc in first 30 sts, work FPhdc around each of next 3 sts, (work BPhdc around each of next 3 sts, work FPhdc around each of next 3 sts) 3 times, sc in last 30 sts.

Row 7: Ch 1, turn; sc in first 3 sc, work FPdc around each of first 2 FPdc one row **below**, sc in next 3 sc, work FPdc around each of next 2 FPdc one row **below**, sc in next 2 sc, † work FPdc around next FPdc one row **below**, sc in next 3 sc, work FPcl around FPcl one row **below**, sc in next 5 sc, work FPcl around FPcl one row **below**, sc in next 3 sc, work FPdc around next FPdc one row **below** †, sc in next 3 sc, work BPhdc around each of next 3 sts, (work FPhdc around each of next 3 sts, work BPhdc around each of next 3 sts) 3 times, sc in next 3 sts, repeat from † to † once, sc in next 2 sc, work FPdc around each of next 2 FPdc one row **below**, sc in next 3 sc, work FPdc around each of next 2 FPdc one row **below**, sc in last 3 sc.

Instructions continued on page 4.

Row 8: Ch 1, turn; sc in first 30 sts, work FPhdc around each of next 3 sts, (work BPhdc around each of next 3 sts, work FPhdc around each of next 3 sts) 3 times, sc in last 30 sts.

Row 9: Ch 1, turn; sc in first 4 sc, work FPdc around each of first 2 FPdc one row **below**, sc in next sc, work FPdc around each of next 2 FPdc one row **below**, † sc in next 3 sc, work FPdc around next FPdc one row **below**, sc in next 2 sc, work FPcl around next FPcl one row **below**, sc in next 3 sc, work Popcorn in next sc, sc in next 3 sc, work FPcl around next FPcl one row **below**, sc in next 2 sc, work FPdc around next FPdc one row **below**, sc in next 3 sc †, work FPhdc around each of next 3 sts, (work BPhdc around each of next 3 sts, work FPhdc around each of next 3 sts) 3 times, repeat from † to † once, work FPdc around each of next 2 FPdc one row **below**, sc in next sc, work FPdc around each of next 2 FPdc one row **below**, sc in last 4 sc.

Row 10: Ch 1, turn; sc in first 30 sts, work BPhdc around each of next 3 sts, (work FPhdc around each of next 3 sts, work BPhdc around each of next 3 sts) 3 times, sc in last 30 sts.

Row 11: Ch 1, turn; sc in first 4 sc, skip first 2 FPdc one row **below**, work FPdc around each of next 2 FPdc, sc in next sc, working in **front** of FPdc just made, work FPdc around each skipped FPdc one row **below**, † sc in next 3 sc, work FPdc around next FPdc one row **below**, sc in next 3 sc, work FPcl around next FPcl one row **below**, sc in next 5 sc, work FPcl around next FPcl one row **below**, sc in next 3 sc, work FPdc around next FPdc one row **below**, sc in next 3 sc †, work FPhdc around each of next 3 sts, (work BPhdc around each of next 3 sts, work FPhdc around each of next 3 sts) 3 times, repeat from † to † once, skip next 2 FPdc one row **below**, work FPdc around each of next 2 FPdc, sc in next sc, working in **front** of FPdc just made, work FPdc around each skipped FPdc one row **below**, sc in last 4 sc.

Row 12: Ch 1, turn; sc in first 30 sts, work FPhdc around each of next 3 sts, (work BPhdc around each of next 3 sts, work FPhdc around each of next 3 sts) 3 times, sc in last 30 sts.

Row 13: Ch 1, turn; sc in first 3 sc, work FPdc around each of first 2 FPdc one row **below**, sc in next 3 sc, work FPdc around each of next 2 FPdc one row **below**, sc in next 2 sc, † work FPdc around next FPdc one row **below**, sc in next 4 sc, work FPcl around next FPcl one row **below**, sc in next 3 sc, work FPcl around next FPcl one row **below**, sc in next 4 sc, work FPdc around next FPdc one row **below** †, sc in next 3 sc, work BPhdc around each of next 3 sts, (work FPhdc around each of next 3 sts, work BPhdc around each of next 3 sts) 3 times, sc in next 3 sc, repeat from † to † once, sc in next 2 sc, work FPdc around each of next 2 FPdc one row **below**, sc in next 3 sc, work FPdc around each of next 2 FPdc one row **below**, sc in last 3 sc.

Row 14: Ch 1, turn; sc in first 30 sts, work FPhdc around each of next 3 sts, (work BPhdc around each of next 3 sts, work FPhdc around each of next 3 sts) 3 times, sc in last 30 sts.

Rows 15-87: Repeat Rows 3-14, 6 times; then repeat Row 3 once **more**.

Finish off.

BACK
Ch 80.

Row 1 (Right side)**:** Sc in second ch from hook and in each ch across: 79 sc.

Note: Mark Row 1 as **right** side.

Row 2: Ch 1, turn; sc in each sc across.

Repeat Row 2 until Back measures same as Front, ending by working a **right** side row; do **not** finish off.

ASSEMBLY

Rnd 1: Ch 1, turn; with **wrong** sides of **both** pieces together, Front facing, matching sts on last row and working through **both** thicknesses, (sc evenly across to next corner, 3 sc in corner) 3 times; insert pillow form, sc evenly across to last corner, 3 sc in last corner; join with slip st to first sc.

Rnd 2: Do **not** turn; working from **left** to **right**, work reverse slip st in each sc around *(Figs. 4a & b, page 23)*; join with slip st to first slip st, finish off.

Center Mock Cable Pillow

Shown on page 8.

■■□□ EASY +

Finished Size: 12¼" (31 cm) square

MATERIALS
Medium Weight Yarn (4)
[7 ounces, 364 yards
(198 grams, 333 meters) per skein]:
  1 skein
Crochet hook, size G (4 mm) **or** size needed
  for gauge
14" (35.5 cm) Square pillow form, knife-edge

GAUGE: 14 sc and 16 rows = 4" (10 cm)

Gauge Swatch: 4" (10 cm) square
Ch 15.
Row 1: Sc in second ch from hook and in each ch across: 14 sc.
Rows 2-16: Ch 1, turn; sc in each sc across. Finish off.

STITCH GUIDE

FRONT POST DOUBLE CROCHET
  (abbreviated FPdc)
YO, working in **front** of previous row, insert hook from **front** to **back** around post of st indicated **(Fig. 3, page 23)**, YO and pull up a loop even with loops on hook (3 loops on hook), (YO and draw through 2 loops on hook) twice. Skip st behind FPdc.

FRONT POST CLUSTER
  (abbreviated FPcl) (uses one st)
★ YO, working in **front** of previous row, insert hook from **front** to **back** around post of st indicated **(Fig. 3, page 23)**, YO and pull up a loop even with loops on hook, YO and draw through 2 loops on hook; repeat from ★ once **more**, YO and draw through all 3 loops on hook. Skip st behind FPcl.

POPCORN (uses one sc)
4 Dc in sc indicated, drop loop from hook, insert hook from **front** to **back** in first dc of 4-dc group, hook dropped loop and draw through st **(Fig. 2, page 23)**.

FRONT
Ch 44.

Row 1 (Right side)**:** Sc in second ch from hook and in each ch across: 43 sc.

Note: Loop a short piece of yarn around any stitch to mark Row 1 as **right** side.

Row 2: Ch 1, turn; sc in each sc across.

Row 3: Ch 1, turn; sc in first 9 sc, † work FPdc around sc one row **below** next sc, (sc in next sc, work FPdc around sc one row **below** next sc) twice †, sc in next 6 sc, work FPcl around sc one row **below** next sc, sc in next sc, work FPcl around sc one row **below** next sc, sc in next 6 sc, repeat from † to † once, sc in last 9 sc.

Row 4 AND ALL WRONG SIDE ROWS: Ch 1, turn; sc in each st across.

Row 5: Ch 1, turn; sc in first 9 sc, † work FPdc around FPdc one row **below** next sc, (sc in next sc, work FPdc around FPdc one row **below** next sc) twice †, sc in next 5 sc, work FPcl around next FPcl 2 rows **below**, sc in next 3 sc, work FPcl around next FPcl 2 rows **below**, sc in next 5 sc, repeat from † to † once, sc in last 9 sc.

Row 7: Ch 1, turn; sc in first 9 sc, † work FPdc around FPdc one row **below** next sc, (sc in next sc, work FPdc around FPdc one row **below** next sc) twice †, sc in next 4 sc, work FPcl around next FPcl 2 rows **below**, sc in next 5 sc, work FPcl around next FPcl 2 rows **below**, sc in next 4 sc, repeat from † to † once, sc in last 9 sc.

Row 9: Ch 1, turn; sc in first 9 sc, † work FPdc around FPdc one row **below** next sc, (sc in next sc, work FPdc around FPdc one row **below** next sc) twice †, sc in next 3 sc, work FPcl around next FPcl 2 rows **below**, sc in next 3 sc, work Popcorn in next sc, sc in next 3 sc, work FPcl around next FPcl 2 rows **below**, sc in next 3 sc, repeat from † to † once, sc in last 9 sc.

Row 11: Ch 1, turn; sc in first 9 sc, † work FPdc around FPdc one row **below** next sc, (sc in next sc, work FPdc around FPdc one row **below** next sc) twice †, sc in next 4 sc, work FPcl around next FPcl 2 rows **below**, sc in next 5 sc, work FPcl around next FPcl 2 rows **below**, sc in next 4 sc, repeat from † to † once, sc in last 9 sc.

Row 13: Ch 1, turn; sc in first 9 sc, † work FPdc around FPdc one row **below** next sc, (sc in next sc, work FPdc around FPdc one row **below** next sc) twice †, sc in next 5 sc, work FPcl around next FPcl 2 rows **below**, sc in next 3 sc, work FPcl around next FPcl 2 rows **below**, sc in next 5 sc, repeat from † to † once, sc in last 9 sc.

Row 15: Ch 1, turn; sc in first 9 sc, † work FPdc around FPdc one row **below** next sc, (sc in next sc, work FPdc around FPdc one row **below** next sc) twice †, sc in next 6 sc, work FPcl around next FPcl 2 rows **below**, sc in next sc, work FPcl around next FPcl 2 rows **below**, sc in next 6 sc, repeat from † to † once, sc in last 9 sc.

Rows 16-51: Repeat Rows 4-15, 3 times.

Finish off.

BACK
Ch 44.

Row 1 (Right side): Sc in second ch from hook and in each ch across: 43 sc.

Note: Mark Row 1 as **right** side.

Row 2: Ch 1, turn; sc in each sc across.

Repeat Row 2 until Back measures same as Front, ending by working a **right** side row; do **not** finish off.

ASSEMBLY
Rnd 1: Ch 1, turn; with **wrong** sides of **both** pieces together, Front facing, matching sts on last row and working through **both** thicknesses, (sc evenly across to next corner, 3 sc in corner) 3 times; insert pillow form, sc evenly across to last corner, 3 sc in last corner; join with slip st to first sc.

Rnd 2: Do **not** turn; working from **left** to **right**, work reverse slip st in each sc around *(Figs. 4a & b, page 23)*; join with slip st to first slip st, finish off.

Snowflake Pillow

Shown on page 9.

EASY +

Finished Size: 13½" (34.5 cm) square

MATERIALS
Medium Weight Yarn (4)
[7 ounces, 364 yards
(198 grams, 333 meters) per skein]:
  1 skein
Crochet hook, size G (4 mm) **or** size needed
  for gauge
14" (35.5 cm) Square pillow form, knife-edge

GAUGE: 14 sc and 16 rows = 4" (10 cm)

Gauge Swatch: 4" (10 cm) square
Ch 15.
Row 1: Sc in second ch from hook and in each ch across: 14 sc.
Rows 2-16: Ch 1, turn; sc in each sc across. Finish off.

STITCH GUIDE

FRONT POST DOUBLE CROCHET
  (abbreviated FPdc)
YO, working in **front** of previous row, insert hook from **front** to **back** around post of st indicated **(Fig. 3, page 23)**, YO and pull up a loop even with loops on hook (3 loops on hook), (YO and draw through 2 loops on hook) twice. Skip sc behind FPdc.

FRONT POST CLUSTER
  (abbreviated FPcl) (uses 5 sc)
YO, working in **front** of previous row, insert hook from **front** to **back** around post of st indicated **(Fig. 3, page 23)**, YO and pull up a loop even with loops on hook (3 loops on hook), YO and draw through 2 loops on hook, ★ YO, skip **next** sc on same row, insert hook from **front** to **back** around post of **next** sc, YO and pull up a loop, YO and draw through 2 loops on hook; repeat from ★ once **more**, YO and draw through all 4 loops on hook. Skip sc behind FPcl.

FRONT
Ch 48.

Row 1 (Right side): Sc in second ch from hook and in each ch across: 47 sc.

Note: Loop a short piece of yarn around any stitch to mark Row 1 as **right** side.

Row 2 AND ALL WRONG SIDE ROWS: Ch 1, turn; sc in each st across.

Row 3: Ch 1, turn; sc in first 3 sc, work FPcl beginning around second sc 2 rows **below**, ★ sc in next 9 sc, skip next 5 sts 2 rows **below** (from last FPcl worked) and work FPcl beginning around next sc; repeat from ★ across to last 3 sc, sc in last 3 sc.

www.leisurearts.com

Row 5: Ch 1, turn; sc in first sc, work FPdc around first FPcl 2 rows **below**, (sc in next sc, work FPdc around same FPcl 2 rows **below**) twice, ★ sc in next 5 sc, work FPdc around next FPcl 2 rows **below**, (sc in next sc, work FPdc around same FPcl 2 rows **below**) twice; repeat from ★ across to last sc, sc in last sc.

Row 7: Ch 1, turn; sc in first 8 sc, work FPcl beginning around seventh st 2 rows **below**, ★ sc in next 9 sc, skip next 5 sts 2 rows **below** (from last FPcl worked) and work FPcl beginning around next sc; repeat from ★ 2 times **more**, sc in last 8 sc.

Row 9: Ch 1, turn; sc in first 6 sc, work FPdc around first FPcl 2 rows **below**, (sc in next sc, work FPdc around same FPcl 2 rows **below**) twice, ★ sc in next 5 sc, work FPdc around next FPcl 2 rows **below**, (sc in next sc, work FPdc around same FPcl 2 rows **below**) twice; repeat from ★ 2 times **more**, sc in last 6 sc.

Rows 10-53: Repeat Rows 2-9, 5 times; then repeat Rows 2-5 once **more**.

Finish off.

BACK
Ch 48.

Row 1 (Right side)**:** Sc in second ch from hook and in each ch across: 47 sc.

Note: Mark Row 1 as **right** side.

Row 2: Ch 1, turn; sc in each sc across.

Repeat Row 2 until Back measures same as Front, ending by working a **right** side row; do **not** finish off.

ASSEMBLY
Rnd 1: Ch 1, turn; with **wrong** sides of **both** pieces together, Front facing, matching sts on last row and working through **both** thicknesses, (sc evenly across to next corner, 3 sc in corner) 3 times; insert pillow form, sc evenly across to last corner, 3 sc in last corner; join with slip st to first sc.

Rnd 2: Do **not** turn; working from **left** to **right**, work reverse slip st in each sc around *(Figs. 4a & b, page 23)*; join with slip st to first slip st, finish off.

Ribbed Pillow

■■□□ EASY +

Finished Size: 12" (30.5 cm) square

MATERIALS
Medium Weight Yarn 🔵4
[7 ounces, 364 yards
(198 grams, 333 meters) per skein]:
  1 skein
Crochet hook, size G (4 mm) **or** size needed
  for gauge
14" (35.5 cm) Square pillow form, knife-edge

GAUGE: 14 sc and 16 rows = 4" (10 cm)

Gauge Swatch: 4" (10 cm) square
Ch 15.
Row 1: Sc in second ch from hook and in each ch across: 14 sc.
Rows 2-16: Ch 1, turn; sc in each sc across.
Finish off.

STITCH GUIDE
FRONT POST DOUBLE CROCHET
  (abbreviated FPdc)
YO, working in **front** of previous row, insert hook from **front** to **back** around post of st indicated *(Fig. 3, page 23)*, YO and pull up a loop even with loops on hook (3 loops on hook), (YO and draw through 2 loops on hook) twice. Skip st behind FPdc.

FRONT
Ch 42.

Row 1 (Right side)**:** Sc in second ch from hook and in each ch across: 41 sc.

Note: Loop a short piece of yarn around any stitch to mark Row 1 as **right** side.

Row 2: Ch 1, turn; sc in each sc across.

Row 3: Ch 1, turn; sc in first 8 sc, work FPdc around sc one row **below** next sc, (sc in next sc, work FPdc around sc one row **below** next sc) twice, ★ sc in next 5 sc, work FPdc around sc one row **below** next sc, (sc in next sc, work FPdc around sc one row **below** next sc) twice; repeat from ★ once **more**, sc in last 8 sc: 32 sc and 9 FPdc.

Row 4: Ch 1, turn; sc in each st across: 41 sc.

Row 5: Ch 1, turn; sc in first 8 sc, work FPdc around FPdc one row **below** next sc, (sc in next sc, work FPdc around FPdc one row **below** next sc) twice, ★ sc in next 5 sc, work FPdc around FPdc one row **below** next sc, (sc in next sc, work FPdc around sc one row **below** next sc) twice; repeat from ★ once **more**, sc in last 8 sc: 32 sc and 9 FPdc.

Rows 6-49: Repeat Rows 4 and 5, 22 times.

Finish off.

www.leisurearts.com

BACK

Ch 42.

Row 1 (Right side): Sc in second ch from hook and in each ch across: 41 sc.

Note: Mark Row 1 as **right** side.

Row 2: Ch 1, turn; sc in each sc across.

Repeat Row 2 until Back measures same as Front, ending by working a **right** side row; do **not** finish off.

ASSEMBLY

Rnd 1: Ch 1, turn; with **wrong** sides of **both** pieces together, Front facing, matching sts on last row and working through **both** thicknesses, (sc evenly across to next corner, 3 sc in corner) 3 times; insert pillow form, sc evenly across to last corner, 3 sc in last corner; join with slip st to first sc.

Rnd 2: Do **not** turn; working from **left** to **right**, work reverse slip st in each st around *(Figs. 4a & b, page 23)*; join with slip st to first slip st, finish off.

Lattice Center Pillow

Shown on page 16.

■■■□ INTERMEDIATE

Finished Size: 22" (56 cm) square

MATERIALS
Medium Weight Yarn (4)
[7 ounces, 364 yards
(198 grams, 333 meters) per skein]:
  3 skeins
Crochet hook, size G (4 mm) **or** size needed
  for gauge
24" (61 cm) Square pillow form, knife-edge

GAUGE: In pattern, 14 sts and
  16 rows (Rows 1-16) = 4" (10 cm)

Gauge Swatch: 4" (10 cm) square
Ch 15.
Rows 1-16: Work same as Front: 14 sts.
Finish off.

✻✻✻

STITCH GUIDE
FRONT POST DOUBLE CROCHET
  (abbreviated FPdc)
YO, working in **front** of previous rows, insert hook from **front** to **back** around post of st indicated *(Fig. 3, page 23)*, YO and pull up a loop even with loops on hook (3 loops on hook), (YO and draw through 2 loops on hook) twice. Skip st behind FPdc.

FRONT
Ch 79.

Row 1 (Right side)**:** Sc in second ch from hook and in each ch across: 78 sc.

Note: Loop a short piece of yarn around any stitch to mark Row 1 as **right** side.

Rows 2-19: Ch 2 **(counts as first hdc, now and throughout)**, turn; slip st in next st, (hdc in next st, slip st in next st) across.

Row 20: Ch 1, turn; sc in each st across.

Row 21: Ch 1, turn; slip st loosely in Front Loop Only of each sc across *(Fig. A)*.

Fig. A

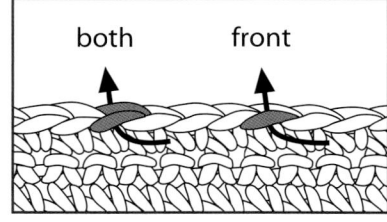

Row 22: Ch 1, turn; working in free loops of sc 2 rows **below** *(Fig. B)*, sc in each sc across.

Fig. B

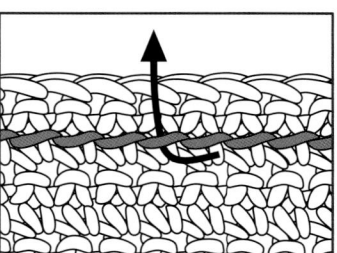

Row 23: Ch 1, turn; working in both loops, sc in first 2 sc, ★ ch 3, skip next 2 sc on previous row, sc in next sc *(Fig. C)*, **turn**, sc in each ch of ch-3 just made *(Fig. D)*, slip st in next sc (at beginning of ch-3) *(Fig. E)*, **turn (Cable made)**, sc in 2 skipped sc **behind** Cable *(Fig. F)*; repeat from ★ across to last sc on previous row, ch 1, sc in last sc: 25 Cables.

Fig. C

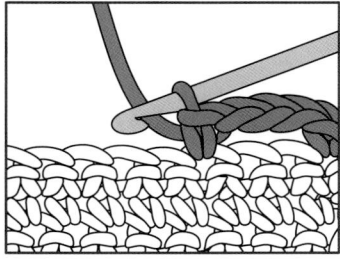

Fig. D

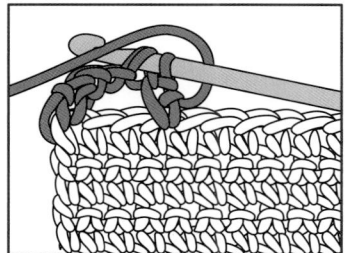

Fig. E

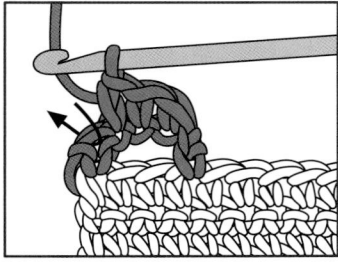

Fig. F

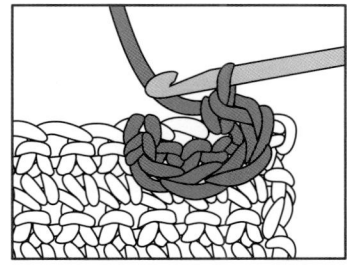

Row 24: Ch 1, turn; sc in first sc, skip next ch, keeping Cables to **right** side and working in sc in **behind** Cables, (2 sc in next sc, sc in next sc) across to last sc, 2 sc in last sc: 78 sc.

Row 25: Ch 1, turn; slip st loosely in Front Loop Only of each sc across.

Row 26: Ch 1, turn; working in free loops of sc 2 rows **below**, sc in each sc across.

Rows 27 and 28: Ch 1, turn; sc in both loops of each sc across.

Row 29: Ch 1, turn; sc in Front Loop Only of each sc across.

Row 30: Ch 1, turn; working in free loops of sc 2 rows **below**, sc in each sc across.

Rows 31 and 32: Ch 1, turn; sc in both loops of each sc across.

Rows 33-38: Repeat Rows 21-26.

Rows 39-42: Ch 1, turn; sc in both loops of each sc across.

Row 43: Ch 1, turn; sc in first 3 sc, work FPdc around second sc 3 rows **below**, ★ skip next 4 sc and work FPdc around next sc, sc in next 4 sc on previous row, work FPdc around sc 3 rows **below** (next to last FPdc made); repeat from ★ across to last 2 sc on previous row, sc in last 2 sc.

Rows 44-46: Ch 1, turn; sc in each st across.

Row 47: Ch 1, turn; sc in first sc, work FPdc around fourth sc 3 rows **below**, sc in next 4 sc on previous row, ★ work FPdc around next sc 3 rows **below** (next to last FPdc made), skip next 4 sc and work FPdc around next sc, sc in next 4 sc on previous row; repeat from ★ across.

Rows 48-50: Ch 1, turn; sc in each st across.

Rows 51-64: Repeat Rows 43-50 once, then repeat Rows 43-48 once **more**.

Rows 65-82: Repeat Rows 21-38.

Rows 83-101: Ch 2, turn; slip st in next st, (hdc in next st, slip st in next st) across.

Row 102: Ch 1, turn; sc in each st across; finish off.

Instructions continued on page 16.

BACK
Ch 79.

Row 1 (Right side): Sc in second ch from hook and in each ch across: 78 sc.

Row 2: Ch 2, turn; slip st in next st, (hdc in next st, slip st in next st) across.

Repeat Row 2 until Back measures same as Front, ending by working a **right** side row; do **not** finish off.

ASSEMBLY
Rnd 1: Ch 1, turn; with **wrong** sides of **both** pieces together, Front facing, matching sts on last row and working through **both** thicknesses, (sc evenly across to next corner, 3 sc in corner) 3 times; insert pillow form, sc evenly across to last corner, 3 sc in last corner; join with slip st to first sc.

Rnd 2: Do **not** turn; working from **left** to **right**, work reverse slip st in each sc around *(Figs. 4a & b, page 23)*; join with slip st to first slip st, finish off.

Two Cable Pillow

Shown on page 17.

EASY +

Finished Size: 12¼" (31 cm) square

MATERIALS
Medium Weight Yarn (4)
[7 ounces, 364 yards
(198 grams, 333 meters) per skein]:
  1 skein
Crochet hook, size G (4 mm) **or** size needed for gauge
14" (35.5 cm) Square pillow form, knife-edge

GAUGE: 14 hdc and 12 rows = 4" (10 cm)

Gauge Swatch: 4" (10 cm) square
Ch 15.
Row 1: Hdc in third ch from hook **(2 skipped chs count as first hdc)** and in each ch across: 14 hdc.
Rows 2-12: Ch 2 **(counts as first hdc)**, turn; hdc in next hdc and in each hdc across.
Finish off.

STITCH GUIDE
FRONT POST TREBLE CROCHET
(abbreviated FPtr)
YO twice, working in **front** of previous row, insert hook from **front** to **back** around post of st indicated *(Fig. A)*, YO and pull up a loop even with loops on hook (4 loops on hook), (YO and draw through 2 loops on hook) 3 times. Skip st behind FPtr.

Fig. A

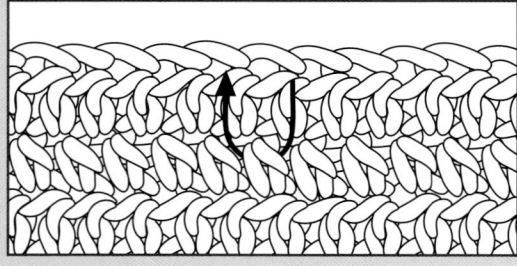

FRONT
Ch 44.

Row 1 (Right side)**:** Hdc in third ch from hook **(2 skipped chs count as first hdc)** and in each ch across: 43 hdc.

Note: Loop a short piece of yarn around any stitch to mark Row 1 as **right** side.

Row 2: Ch 2 **(counts as first hdc, now and throughout)**, turn; hdc in next hdc and in each hdc across.

Row 3: Ch 2, turn; hdc in next 8 hdc, † work FPtr around hdc one row **below** each of next 2 hdc, hdc in next hdc, work FPtr around hdc one row **below** each of next 2 hdc †, hdc in next 15 hdc, repeat from † to † once, hdc in last 9 hdc.

Row 4 AND ALL WRONG SIDE ROWS: Ch 2, turn; hdc in next st and in each st across.

Row 5: Ch 2, turn; hdc in next 8 hdc, † skip next 2 FPtr 2 rows **below**, work FPtr around each of next 2 FPtr, hdc in next hdc, working in **front** of FPtr just made, work FPtr around each of 2 skipped FPtr †, hdc in next 15 hdc, repeat from † to † once, hdc in last 9 hdc.

Row 7: Ch 2, turn; hdc in next 7 hdc, † work FPtr around each of next 2 FPtr 2 rows **below**, hdc in next 3 hdc, work FPtr around each of next 2 FPtr 2 rows **below** †, hdc in next 13 hdc, repeat from † to † once, hdc in last 8 hdc.

Row 9: Ch 2, turn; hdc in next 6 hdc, † work FPtr around each of next 2 FPtr 2 rows **below**, hdc in next 5 hdc, work FPtr around each of next 2 FPtr 2 rows **below** †, hdc in next 11 hdc, repeat from † to † once, hdc in last 7 hdc.

Row 11: Ch 2, turn; hdc in next 7 hdc, † work FPtr around each of next 2 FPtr 2 rows **below**, hdc in next 3 hdc, work FPtr around each of next 2 FPtr 2 rows **below** †, hdc in next 13 hdc, repeat from † to † once, hdc in last 8 hdc.

Row 13: Ch 2, turn; hdc in next 8 hdc, † work FPtr around next 2 FPtr 2 rows **below**, hdc in next hdc, work FPtr next 2 FPtr 2 rows **below** †, hdc in next 15 hdc, repeat from † to † once, hdc in last 9 hdc.

Rows 14-36: Repeat Rows 4-13 twice, then repeat Rows 4-6 once **more**.

Row 37: Ch 2, turn; hdc in next 8 hdc, † work FPtr around next 2 FPtr 2 rows **below**, hdc in next hdc, work FPtr next 2 FPtr 2 rows **below** †, hdc in next 15 hdc, repeat from † to † once, hdc in last 9 hdc; finish off.

BACK
Ch 44.

Row 1 (Right side)**:** Hdc in third ch from hook **(2 skipped chs count as first hdc)** and in each ch across: 43 hdc.

Note: Mark Row 1 as **right** side.

Row 2: Ch 2, turn; hdc in next hdc and in each hdc across.

Repeat Row 2 until Back measures same as Front, ending by working a **right** side row; do **not** finish off.

ASSEMBLY
Rnd 1: Ch 1, turn; with **wrong** sides of **both** pieces together, Front facing, matching sts on last row and working through **both** thicknesses, (sc evenly across to next corner, 3 sc in corner) 3 times; insert pillow form, sc evenly across to last corner, 3 sc in last corner; join with slip st to first sc.

Rnd 2: Do **not** turn; working from **left** to **right**, work reverse slip st in each sc around *(Figs. 4a & b, page 23)*; join with slip st to first slip st, finish off.

Basketweave Pillow

Shown on page 21.

■■□□ EASY +

Finished Size: 11" (28 cm) square

MATERIALS
Medium Weight Yarn (4)
[7 ounces, 364 yards
(198 grams, 333 meters) per skein]:
 1 skein
Crochet hook, size G (4 mm) **or** size needed
 for gauge
12" (30.5 cm) Square pillow form, knife-edge

GAUGE: In pattern, 15 sts = 4" (10 cm) and
 9 rows = $3^{3}/_{4}$" (9.5 cm)

Gauge Swatch: $4^{3}/_{4}$"w x 4"h (12 cm x 10 cm)
Ch 19.
Rows 1-10: Work same as Front: 18 sts.
Finish off.

✳✳✳

STITCH GUIDE
FRONT POST DOUBLE CROCHET (abbreviated FPdc)
YO, insert hook from **front** to **back** around post of st indicated **(Fig. 1, page 23)**, YO and pull up a loop even with loops on hook (3 loops on hook), (YO and draw through 2 loops on hook) twice.

BACK POST DOUBLE CROCHET (abbreviated BPdc)
YO, insert hook from **back** to **front** around post of st indicated **(Fig. 1, page 23)**, YO and pull up a loop even with loops on hook (3 loops on hook), (YO and draw through 2 loops on hook) twice.

FRONT
Ch 43.

Row 1 (Right side)**:** Sc in second ch from hook and in each ch across: 42 sc.

Note: Loop a short piece of yarn around any stitch to mark Row 1 as **right** side.

Row 2: Ch 3 **(counts as first dc, now and throughout)**, turn; dc in next sc and in each sc across.

Row 3: Ch 2 **(counts as first hdc, now and throughout)**, turn; (work FPdc around each of next 4 sts, work BPdc around each of next 4 sts) across to last dc, hdc in last dc.

Rows 4 and 5: Ch 2, turn; (work FPdc around each of next 4 sts, work BPdc around each of next 4 sts) across to last hdc, hdc in last hdc.

www.leisurearts.com

Rows 6-8: Ch 2, turn; (work BPdc around each of next 4 sts, work FPdc around each of next 4 sts) across to last hdc, hdc in last hdc.

Rows 9-11: Ch 2, turn; (work FPdc around each of next 4 sts, work BPdc around each of next 4 sts) across to last hdc, hdc in last hdc.

Rows 12-26: Repeat Rows 6-11 twice, then repeat Rows 6-8 once **more**.

Finish off.

BACK
Ch 42.

Row 1 (Right side)**:** Dc in fourth ch from hook **(3 skipped chs count as first dc)** and in each ch across: 40 dc.

Note: Mark Row 1 as **right** side.

Row 2: Ch 3, turn; dc in next dc and in each dc across.

Repeat Row 2 until Back measures same as Front, ending by working a **right** side row; do **not** finish off.

ASSEMBLY

Rnd 1: Ch 1, turn; with **wrong** sides of **both** pieces together, Front facing, matching sts on last row and working through **both** thicknesses, (sc evenly across to next corner, 3 sc in corner) 3 times; insert pillow form, sc evenly across to last corner, 3 sc in last corner; join with slip st to first sc.

Rnd 2: Do **not** turn; working from **left** to **right**, work reverse slip st in each sc around *(Figs. 4a & b, page 23)*; join with slip st to first slip st, finish off.

General Instructions

ABBREVIATIONS

BPdc	Back Post double crochet(s)
BPhdc	Back Post half double crochet(s)
ch(s)	chain(s)
cm	centimeters
FPcl	Front Post cluster(s)
FPdc	Front Post double crochet(s)
FPhdc	Front Post half double crochet(s)
FPtr	Front Post treble crochet(s)
hdc	half double crochet(s)
mm	millimeters
Rnd(s)	Round(s)
sc	single crochet(s)
st(s)	stitch(es)
YO	yarn over

★ — work instructions following ★ as many **more** times as indicated in addition to the first time.

† to † — work all instructions from first † to second † **as many** times as specified.

( ) or [ ] — work enclosed instructions **as many** times as specified by the number immediately following **or** contains explanatory remarks.

colon (:) — the number(s) given after a colon at the end of a row or round denote(s) the number of stitches or spaces you should have on that row or round.

GAUGE

Exact gauge is **essential** for proper size. Before beginning your project, make the sample swatch given in the individual instructions in the yarn and hook specified. After completing the swatch, measure it, counting your stitches and rows or round carefully. If your swatch is larger or smaller than specified, **make another, changing hook size to get the correct gauge**. Keep trying until you find the size hook that will give you the specified gauge.

CROCHET TERMINOLOGY

UNITED STATES		INTERNATIONAL
slip stitch (slip st)	=	single crochet (sc)
single crochet (sc)	=	double crochet (dc)
half double crochet (hdc)	=	half treble crochet (htr)
double crochet (dc)	=	treble crochet (tr)
treble crochet (tr)	=	double treble crochet (dtr)
double treble crochet (dtr)	=	triple treble crochet (ttr)
triple treble crochet (tr tr)	=	quadruple treble crochet (qtr)
skip	=	miss

Yarn Weight Symbol & Names	LACE 0	SUPER FINE 1	FINE 2	LIGHT 3	MEDIUM 4	BULKY 5	SUPER BULKY 6
Type of Yarns in Category	Fingering, 10-count crochet thread	Sock, Fingering Baby	Sport, Baby	DK, Light Worsted	Worsted, Afghan, Aran	Chunky, Craft, Rug	Bulky, Roving
Crochet Gauge* Ranges in Single Crochet to 4" (10 cm)	32-42 double crochets**	21-32 sts	16-20 sts	12-17 sts	11-14 sts	8-11 sts	5-9 sts
Advised Hook Size Range	Steel*** 6,7,8 Regular hook B-1	B-1 to E-4	E-4 to 7	7 to I-9	I-9 to K-10.5	K-10.5 to M-13	M-13 and larger

*GUIDELINES ONLY: The chart above reflects the most commonly used gauges and hook sizes for specific yarn categories.

** Lace weight yarns are usually crocheted on larger-size hooks to create lacy openwork patterns. Accordingly, a gauge range is difficult to determine. Always follow the gauge stated in your pattern.

*** Steel crochet hooks are sized differently from regular hooks—the higher the number the smaller the hook, which is the reverse of regular hook sizing.

CROCHET HOOKS

U.S.	B-1	C-2	D-3	E-4	F-5	G-6	H-8	I-9	J-10	K-10½	N	P	Q
Metric - mm	2.25	2.75	3.25	3.5	3.75	4	5	5.5	6	6.5	9	10	15

HINTS

As in all crocheted pieces, good finishing techniques make a big difference in the quality of the piece. Make a habit of taking care of loose ends as you work. Thread a yarn needle with the yarn end. With **wrong** side facing, weave the needle through several stitches, then reverse the direction and weave it back through several stitches. When ends are secure, clip them off close to work.

POST STITCH

Work around the post of stitch indicated, inserting the hook in the direction of arrow *(Fig. 1)*.

Fig. 1

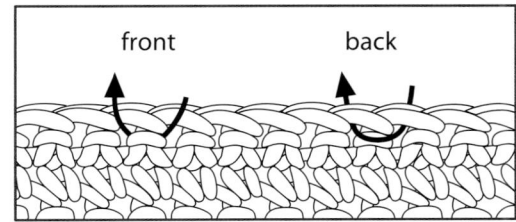

POPCORN (uses one sc)

Work 4 dc in sc indicated, drop loop from hook, insert hook from **front** to **back** in first dc of 4-dc group, hook dropped loop and draw through st *(Fig. 2)*.

Fig. 2

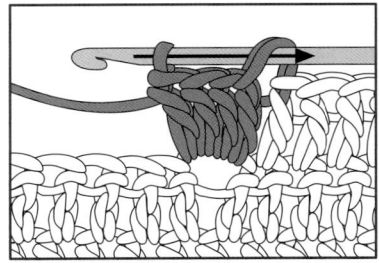

WORKING IN FRONT OF PREVIOUS ROW

Working in **front** of previous row, insert the hook from **front** to **back** around the post of stitch indicated *(Fig. 3)*.

Fig. 3

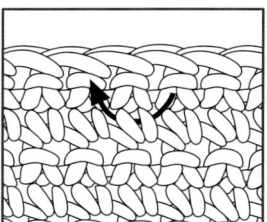

REVERSE SLIP STITCH

Working from **left** to **right**, insert hook in st to right of hook *(Fig. 4a)*, YO and draw through st **and** through loop on hook *(Fig. 4b)*.

Fig. 4a

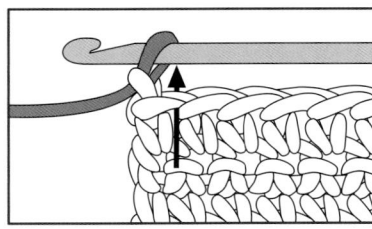

Fig. 4b

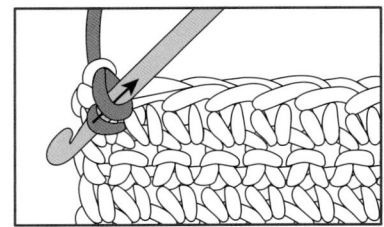

■□□□ BEGINNER	Projects for first-time crocheters using basic stitches. Minimal shaping.
■■□□ EASY	Projects using yarn with basic stitches, repetitive stitch patterns, simple color changes, and simple shaping and finishing.
■■■□ INTERMEDIATE	Projects using a variety of techniques, such as basic lace patterns or color patterns, mid-level shaping and finishing.
■■■■ EXPERIENCED	Projects with intricate stitch patterns, techniques and dimension, such as non-repeating patterns, multi-color techniques, fine threads, small hooks, detailed shaping and refined finishing.

Yarn Information

Each Pillow in this leaflet was made using Red Heart® Super Saver® yarn #313 Aran. Any brand of Medium Weight Yarn may be used. It is best to refer to the yardage/meters when determining how many balls or skeins to purchase. Remember, to arrive at the finished size, it is the GAUGE/TENSION that is important, not the brand of yarn.

✻✻✻✻✻✻✻✻✻✻✻✻✻✻✻✻✻✻✻✻✻✻✻✻✻✻✻✻✻✻✻✻✻✻✻✻

We have made every effort to ensure that these instructions are accurate and complete. We cannot, however, be responsible for human error, typographical mistakes, or variations in individual work.

Production Team: Writer/Technical Editor - Linda Daley; Editorial Writer - Susan McManus Johnson; Senior Graphic Artist - Lora Puls; Graphic Artists - Jacob Casleton, Becca Snider, and Janie Wright; Photography by BPD Studios www.bpdstudios.com

For digital downloads of Leisure Arts' best-selling designs, visit http://www.leisureartslibrary.com

Copyright © 2011 by Leisure Arts, Inc., 5701 Ranch Drive, Little Rock, AR 72223. All rights reserved. This publication is protected under federal copyright laws. Reproduction or distribution of this publication or any other Leisure Arts publication, including publications which are out of print, is prohibited unless specifically authorized. This includes, but is not limited to, any form of reproduction or distribution on or through the Internet, including posting, scanning, or e-mail transmission.